MOSES AND PAUL

The Dispensers of Law and Grace

By Cornelius R. Stam

MOSES AND PAUL

The Dispensers of Law and Grace

By

Cornelius R. Stam

Founder of the Berean Bible Society
and
Prolific Author of over Thirty Bible Study Books,
Including the Classic Work: Things That Differ

BEREAN BIBLE SOCIETY
N112 W17761 Mequon Road
Germantown, WI 53022
(Metro Milwaukee)

Copyright, 1956

by

BEREAN BIBLE SOCIETY
N112 W17761 Mequon Road
Germantown, WI 53022

Tenth Printing 2012

ISBN: 1-893874-09-5

Printed in the United States of America

WORZALLA PUBLISHING COMPANY
STEVENS POINT, WISCONSIN

Cover Photos: ©iStockphoto.com/Amanda Rohde
©iStockphoto.com/John Said

CONTENTS

"For I speak to you Gentiles, inasmuch as I am the apostle of the Gentiles; I magnify mine office"(Rom. 11:13).

"But I certify you, brethren, that the gospel which was preached of me is not after man.
"For I neither received it of man, neither was I taught it, but by the revelation of Jesus Christ" (Gal. 1:11,12).

INTRODUCTION

$\mathfrak{T}$hose who have not yet come to understand the distinctive character of Paul's message and apostleship frequently complain that we make too much of him. To put it in the words of one critic: "In the Roman Catholic Church it is *Mary, Mary, Mary*; among these 'grace' people it is *Paul, Paul, Paul.*"

One result of this criticism is that some who *do* see quite clearly that Paul was divinely appointed to usher in the present dispensation of grace, begin to refer with apologies and qualifications to those passages wherein Paul himself insists upon his apostolic commission and authority, and so they fall, and cause others to fall, into the same trap which has so long crippled and bound the Church: the confusion of the message and program committed to

Paul with that previously committed to the twelve.

The simple *fact* is that while Fundamentalists generally, along with Modernists and Roman Catholics, have considered Paul as merely one of the apostles, entrusted with the same message the twelve were sent to proclaim, the *Scriptures* clearly teach that *this is not so*; that his message and ministry were *distinct* and *separate* from theirs; that to him was committed the doctrine and the program for a *new* dispensation never before even contemplated, except in the mind of God.

The failure to recognize this fact, we say, is the basic cause of the confusion and division which have gripped the Church for so many centuries.

Perhaps the distinctiveness of Paul's ministry can be best understood and appreciated if we compare it with that of Moses, especially as he himself discusses it in Deuteronomy 4.

This we sought to do in a series of articles published in the *Berean Searchlight* in 1952. At that time the response from our readers was so encouraging, and so many have since urged us to publish them in book form, that we have felt led to do so and now send this volume forth with the prayer that the Holy Spirit will use it to enlighten many of His people and bring them into fields of greater blessing and usefulness.

Cornelius R. Stam

Chicago, Illinois
August 20, 1956

CHAPTER I

Pauline Authority

No apology whatever is due for obeying the written Word of God, rightly divided, and it was *by inspiration of God*, not from pride or self-importance, that the apostle declared:

"For I speak to you Gentiles, inasmuch as I am the apostle of the Gentiles; *I magnify mine office*" (Rom. 11:13).

Indeed, the sad condition of the Church through the greater part of the present dispensation has been directly due to her disobedience to this passage of Scripture and to her almost constant rebellion against the God-given authority of Paul as the Apostle of the Gentiles.

It is true that in our preaching and teaching of the Word we probably refer to Paul more often than to any other human being except our Lord Jesus Christ, who was both God and Man. It must not be concluded from this, however, that we consider Paul to be even nearly as great as Christ, or place the two at all on the same level.

We know that Paul was the chief of sinners, saved by grace, while Christ was the holy Son of God and the Savior of sinners. We know that Paul was *nothing* in himself, while Christ is *everything*, for *"In Him dwelleth all the fullness of the Godhead bodily"* (Col. 2:9). But it was to Paul that the glorified Lord committed the revelation of His message and program for us in this present dispensation.

It is not the *person* but the *position* of Paul that we magnify even as the Scriptures do, and did we yield to the constant clamor of those who minimize, rather than magnify, Paul's office, we should be as disobedient to the truth as they, and also as confused.

12

Paul rebuked the Corinthians for their carnality, saying: *"Every one of you saith, I am of Paul; and I of Apollos; and I of Cephas; and I of Christ. Is Christ divided?"* (I Cor. 1:12,13). *"For while one saith, I am of Paul; and another, I am of Apollos; are ye not carnal? Who then is Paul, and who is Apollos, but ministers BY whom ye believed, even as the Lord gave to every man?"* (I Cor. 3:4,5).

Yet after all this the apostle twice urged these *same* Corinthians: *"Be ye followers of me"* (I Cor. 4:16; 11:1). Was he contradicting himself here? Did he mean that it was carnal to favor Apollos or Cephas or Christ, but spiritual to favor Paul? No indeed. The point is that the Corinthians had begun to turn their backs upon the revelation given to Paul for the Gentiles and had taken sides, some with Paul, some with Apollos, some with Cephas and some with Christ, *as though these were working in opposition to, or at least in competition with each other.* This was not the case, for the same risen Lord who had sent Peter forth to proclaim His kingdom rights, later raised up Paul to go forth with the message of grace. Peter and the others at Jerusalem had recognized this and, rather than opposing Paul, had solemnly and publicly acknowledged his position by extending to him the right hand of fellowship (Gal. 2:7-9). Thus there was full agreement between them as to the further revelation committed to Paul as there was also between Paul and Apollos (See Acts 18:26; I Cor. 3:6; 4:6; 16:12). In a word, it was not a question of personalities, but of *a divine revelation and a God-given position.* This should be clearly understood, and no apologies should ever be made for acknowledging the spiritual authority of the Apostle Paul over believers today.

When Israel wandered from God, in days of old, it was not merely because she rebelled against the Word of God in general, but because she rebelled against the Word of God *through Moses* in particular and in

14

the revival under Ezra, for example, the people were not called upon to follow programs in force in former dispensations, but were exhorted to return in obedience to *the law of Moses*. Did this exalt Moses above God? In no wise, for Moses' authority was not inherent; it was *delegated* to him by God.

Just so the present deplorable condition of the Church is due, not merely to rebellion against the Word of God in general, but to rebellion against the Word of God *through Paul* in particular. Nor does God now call upon us to go back to programs in force in former dispensations, but to follow, in obedience, the program of grace, for, remember, as surely as *the dispensation of the law* was committed to Moses, so surely was *the dispensation of the grace of God* later committed to Paul, as he says in Ephesians 3:1-3:

"For this cause I Paul, the prisoner of Jesus Christ for you Gentiles,

"If ye have heard of *the dispensation of the grace of God* which is given me to you-ward:

"How that by revelation He made known unto me the mystery...."

We have often felt that those who find it difficult to understand Paul's unique position as the apostle of grace, would be helped by an examination of Moses' position in comparison. We therefore submit this brief study of the fourth chapter of Deuteronomy, in which Moses probably has most to say about his commission and authority.

CHAPTER II

The Personal Elements in the Pauline Epistles

Those who are disturbed by the pronounced personal element in Paul's epistles should certainly take the time to read the five books of Moses, for while Paul refers to himself by name some thirty times and by the personal pronoun several hundred times in his epistles, Moses refers to himself by name more than six hundred times and by the personal pronoun several thousand times in his writings. The writings of Moses are, to be sure, considerably more voluminous than those of Paul, but even proportionately Moses refers to himself far more often than does Paul, emphasizing again and again his God-given authority over the people of Israel. In Deuteronomy 4:1,2 we have a typical example:

"Now therefore hearken, O Israel, unto the statutes and unto the judgments *which I teach you*, for to do them, that ye may live, and go in and possess the land which the Lord God of your fathers giveth you.

"Ye shall not add unto the word *which I command you*, neither shall ye diminish ought from it, that ye may keep the commandments of the Lord your God *which I command you*."

Why did Moses here place all this emphasis upon himself? Was this due to human pride or self-importance? It was not, for we read in Numbers 12:3 the Spirit-inspired statement:

"Now the man Moses was very meek, above all the men which were upon the face of the earth."

As we learn from Hebrews 3:2, Moses was "faithful to Him that appointed him." Though nothing in himself, Moses had been chosen and commissioned by God to dispense the law to Israel, and His God-given message was not to be confused with the words of other men of God. He was not to be considered merely a godly man, worthy of an equal hearing with others. He was *the* man, the *one* man, to whom God had originally committed the dispensation of the law, and to confuse *his* words with those of others would have been to obscure God's message and program for that day.

The Lord Jesus, while on earth, amply confirmed Moses in this emphasis upon his God-given position.

After cleansing a leper, the Lord *"straitly [strictly] charged him, and forthwith sent him away;*

"And saith unto him, See thou say nothing to any man: but go thy way, show thyself to the priest, and offer for thy cleansing *those things which Moses commanded,* **for a testimony unto them" (Mark 1:43,44).**

When the Pharisees brought up the question of divorce, He asked them in reply:

"...What did Moses command you?" **(Mark 10:3).**

Denouncing the scribes and Pharisees for their wickedness, He nevertheless insisted:

"...The scribes and the Pharisees sit in Moses' seat:

"All therefore whatsoever they bid you observe, that observe and do..." **(Matt. 23:2,3).**

So with Paul. He did not claim to be anything in himself. He called himself *the chief of sinners* (I Tim. 1:15), *"less than the least of all saints"* (Eph. 3:8) and *"not worthy to be called an apostle"* (I Cor. 15:9) but God had originally committed to *him*, to him *alone*, the dispensation of His grace and the divine program for the age in which we now live. Indeed, he himself was the supreme *example* of the grace he was sent forth to proclaim (I Tim. 1:12-16) so that if his apostleship could be called in question, so could the message he proclaimed. He was therefore accountable to God to make all this clear to others, so that the divine message and program might not be confused with what had gone before.

This is the reason for Paul's repeated references to himself and his vigorous defense of his own apostleship. This is why, by inspiration of God, he made such strong statements as the following:

"But though we, or an angel from heaven, preach any other gospel unto you than that which we have preached unto you, *let him be accursed.*

"As we said before, so say I now again, If any man preach any other gospel unto you than that ye have received, *let him be accursed*"[1] **(Gal. 1:8,9).**

---

1. The professing Church has largely *obscured* the great Pauline message by *confusing* it with divine instructions for *other* dispensations. Even this has been attended by God's curse instead of His blessing, and no amount of trying to restore the blessing will avail, apart from a recovery of the pure, unadulterated message and program which God, by revelation, committed to Paul for us.

CHAPTER III

How Paul Received His Authority

Moses did not personally decide to impose laws upon Israel. He was appointed by God Himself to be Israel's great law-giver. He points this out again and again, and nowhere more clearly than in this fourth chapter of Deuteronomy:

"Behold, I have taught you statutes and judgments, *even as the Lord my God commanded me....*"

"*And the Lord commanded me* at that time to teach you statutes and judgments..." (Deut. 4:5,14).

Nor did God appoint Moses by some indirect method, as by a subjective vision or dream, but by personally appearing and speaking with him, as we learn from Exodus and Numbers.

"And the Lord spake unto Moses face to face, as a man speaketh unto his friend..." (Ex. 33:11).

"And [the Lord] said, Hear now My words: If there be a prophet among you, I the Lord will make Myself known unto him in a vision, and will speak unto him in a dream.

"My servant Moses is not so, who is faithful in all Mine house.

"With him will I speak mouth to mouth, even apparently,[1] and not in dark speeches; and the similitude of the Lord shall he behold: wherefore then were ye not afraid to speak against My servant Moses?

"And the anger of the Lord was kindled against them; and He departed" (Num. 12:6-9).

From the latter passage above it is evident that the directness of Moses' appointment by God Himself put him in a very different category from others to whom God had revealed Himself indirectly by visions, dreams, etc., for here Moses' own

1. *Plainly.*

24

brother and sister are sternly rebuked for questioning Moses' unique authority. They were rebelling against *God* when they rebelled against the one whom He had personally and directly appointed. Hence the Lord asked them: *"Wherefore then were ye not afraid to speak against My servant Moses?"* and so saying, He departed from them in anger.

The argument for Pauline authority today is fully as strong. Paul did not appoint himself the apostle of the Gentiles, or invent the message he proclaimed to them. In his Spirit-inspired writings he uses practically the same phraseology as did Moses.

Concerning the Lord's Supper he says:

"For I have received of the Lord that which also I delivered unto you..." **(I Cor. 11:23).**

Concerning the gospel which he preached among the Gentiles he says:

"For I delivered unto you first of all that which I also received..." **(I Cor. 15:3).**

25

Concerning the Lord's coming to catch up His own, he says:

"For this we say unto you by the word of the Lord..." (I Thes. 4:15).

And Paul, like Moses, received his commission and authority *directly* from the glorified Lord Himself, not by some indirect method. *How fully* either Moses or Paul was permitted to see the Lord in His glory is not the question here. The point is that neither saw Him merely in a subjective vision or dream, but by direct revelation. Hence in his letter to the Galatians Paul emphatically states:

"But I certify you, brethren, that the gospel which was preached of me is not after man.

"For I neither received it of man, neither was I taught it, but by the revelation of Jesus Christ" (Gal. 1:11,12).

Mark well, he did not receive his message by a revelation *from* Christ, merely, but by *the revelation OF Christ to him.*

As it had been with Moses, so it was with Paul; the Lord revealed *Himself* to him and spoke with him face to face and mouth to mouth, only, the One who had appeared to Moses with the Law, amid the lightnings and thunders of Sinai, had since been manifested in the flesh to die for sin and now appeared to Paul with a message of infinite grace.

As with Moses, it was not once, but again and again that the Lord appeared to Paul to speak with him face to face and mouth to mouth. In the account of his conversion given before Agrippa, he tells how he had *"heard a voice speaking"* to him, and how the Lord had said to him:

"...I have appeared unto thee for this purpose, to make thee a minister and a witness both of these things which thou hast seen, and of those things in the which I will appear unto thee" (Acts 26:16).

One of these times in which the Lord was again to appear to him was upon his first return to Jerusalem after his conversion. He tells about it himself:

27

"And it came to pass, that, when I was come again to Jerusalem, even while I prayed in the temple, I was in a trance;[2]

"*And saw Him saying unto me,* Make haste, and get thee quickly out of Jerusalem: for they will not receive thy testimony concerning Me" (Acts 22:17,18).

So the Lord appeared to Paul again and spoke to him face to face and mouth to mouth, this time commanding him to depart from Jerusalem because his testimony to Israel would now be futile. God had dealt with Israel for a long time, but now the spiritual crisis had come. Stephen had been stoned to death and God had raised up Paul to go forth as *another* apostle, to bring *another* message to a world of lost sinners: *"the gospel of the grace of God."*

In his second letter to the Corinthians the apostle relates how upon one occasion he had actually been *"caught up to the third heaven,"* had *seen the Lord* and

_____
2. Gr. *Ekstasis.*

had *"heard unspeakable words"* (II Cor. 12:1-4). Indeed, in this same passage he speaks of *"the abundance"* of the revelations (Ver. 7) and he says, regarding the future: *"I will come to visions and revelations of the Lord"* (Ver. 1).

These repeated revelations of the Lord Himself to the apostle give us the assurance that in the epistles of Paul we may find the particular truths, both spiritual and practical, which concern us as members of the Body of Christ, and the particular message which we are to proclaim to the world about us.

It gives us confidence that we are preaching God's message for sinners today when we declare:

"To him that worketh not, but believeth on Him that justifieth the ungodly, his faith is counted for righteousness" (Rom. 4:5).

"Being justified freely by His grace through the redemption that is in Christ Jesus" (Rom. 3:24).

29

It gives us confidence that we are in the will of God in our determination to stand fast in liberty and allow God's grace to do its work in our lives.

Today we are not to be subject to Moses, for God Himself has set the covenant of the law aside. Nor are we to be subject to the twelve, as the Pentecostal church was, for the ministry of the twelve was superseded by that of Paul upon Israel's rejection of Christ as King. Today we are to conform our teachings and practices to the great revelation committed by the glorified Lord to the Apostle Paul. The *whole* Word of God, of course, is for our profit, but all must be viewed in the light of this.

CHAPTER IV

The Importance of Strict Obedience to Pauline Authority

We have seen in the case of Moses that he was not to be considered merely *another* godly man who deserved an equal hearing with others. He was *the* man, the *one* man, to whom God had committed the dispensation of the law, and every other man of God for the fifteen hundred years that followed had to take his place under Moses, so that even Christ on earth was obedient to Moses' law and taught His followers to be (Matt. 23:1-3).

As we have seen, there was one occasion when Miriam and Aaron, Moses' sister and brother, complained—apparently at the provocation of Miriam:

"...Hath the Lord indeed spoken only by Moses? Hath He not spoken also by us?..." (Num. 12:2).

For this *"the anger of the Lord was kindled against them"* (12:9). Miriam was smitten with leprosy (12:10) and even though, upon the confession and intercession of Aaron, she was restored, she was made to be *"ashamed"* and *"shut out from the camp seven days"* (12:14).

Later Korah, Dathan and Abiram, with "two hundred and fifty princes...famous in the congregation, men of renown" (Num. 16:2) gathered themselves together against Moses, complaining that he and Aaron had taken too much upon them and had lifted themselves up above the congregation of the Lord (16:3). But at God's command Moses had his critics stand together in a company and said to them: *"Hereby ye shall know that the Lord hath sent me to do all these works; for I have not done them of mine own mind"* (16:28).

"And it came to pass, as he had made an end of speaking all these words, that the ground clave asunder that was under them:

"And the earth opened her mouth, and swallowed them up, and their houses, and all the men that appertained unto Korah, and all their goods" (16:31,32).

It is fortunate for most believers today that this is the dispensation of grace rather than of law, for how many, alas, have rebelled against the God-ordained authority of Paul as His apostle for this age! How many, even among Fundamentalists, have fallen into the sin of the Corinthians and keep forever comparing Paul's merits with those of the other apostles or with those of Christ, arguing: "Was Paul so much better or greater than the other apostles?" and, "Which are more important, the words of Jesus or the words of Paul?" Frequently such people feel they have won a great victory when they quote to us the words of Paul himself:

"If any man teach otherwise, and consent not to wholesome words, even the words of our Lord Jesus Christ, and to the doctrine which is according to godliness; He is proud, knowing nothing, but doting

about questions...from such withdraw thyself" (I Tim. 6:3-5).

But first let us inquire why these critics thus compare "the words of Jesus" with those of Paul, and why they quote the above passage to us. Is it because they are so sincerely desirous of *obeying* the words which the Lord Jesus spoke while on earth? It is not, for they constantly *disobey* them, from the "Sermon on the Mount" to the "Great Commission." Do they sell what they have and give alms? (Luke 12:33). Do they refrain from laying up treasures on earth? (Matt. 6:19). Do they take no thought for the morrow? (Matt. 6:34). They do not quote I Timothy 6:3 to us because they really mean to *obey* the words of Christ on earth, but because they are determined to minimize what God has magnified: the office of Paul as the apostle of the Gentiles (Rom. 11:13).

Even a superficial examination of I Timothy 6:3-5 should show them that far from supporting them in their contention, this passage proves a boomerang to them, for it is in connection with the instructions which *Paul*, by the Spirit, had given to Timothy, that he wrote:

"If any man teach OTHERWISE, and consent not to...the words of our Lord Jesus Christ...he is proud," etc.

In other words, the apostle is here insisting that his words are *"the words of the Lord Jesus"* and that therefore it is the more serious to disobey them. The apostle writes in the same vein to the carnal Corinthians who had belittled his apostolic authority, comparing him with Apollos, Cephas and Christ:

"...If I come again, I will not spare: *since ye seek a proof of Christ speaking in me...*" (II Cor. 13:2,3).

Those who, like the Corinthians, would minimize the office of Paul, should learn that it is not a question of personalities but of *a message and a program* committed by the glorified Lord *to one man—Paul—for us*, for as they fail to recognize

Paul's God-given authority they also fail to glorify Christ as they ought, for it was to and through Paul that the absent Lord revealed His infinite glory at the Father's right hand. It is Paul, and no one until Paul, who says:

"Wherefore henceforth know we no man after the flesh: yea, though we have known Christ after the flesh, yet now henceforth know we Him no more" **(II Cor. 5:16).**

The point to be remembered, then, is that it is not a question of personalities; of who is greater, Peter or Paul or Christ (for Christ is not to be compared with fallen man) but of the simple fact that the risen, exalted Lord, *after* His earthly ministry and His commission to the twelve; after Israel's rejection of the Pentecostal message, raised up *another* apostle and committed to him the message and the program for the day in which we live.

From this we conclude that it is our solemn responsibility to pay particular attention to the Word of God *through Paul,* in order that we may understand it thoroughly and obey it fully.

In his message to the people of Israel Moses said:

"Ye shall not add unto the word which I command you, neither shall ye diminish ought from it, that ye may keep the commandments of the Lord your God which I command you" (Deut. 4:2).

It was not enough to "get the gist" of Moses' words and to carry them out "in substance." They were to be obeyed to the letter. Similarly we are to carry out in detail the program outlined for us by the Apostle Paul, for he likewise says, by the Spirit:

"Hold fast *the form of sound words*, which thou hast heard of me, in faith and love which is in Christ Jesus" (II Tim. 1:13).

Today it would be *disobedience* to place ourselves under the law of Moses, for spiritual authority is no longer vested in Moses, but in *Paul*, and Paul informed the Galatians of this in no uncertain terms.

The Galatians, after having come to know Christ through Paul's "preaching of the cross," had begun to submit themselves to the law of Moses. They had not meant to be disobedient. They had not indulged in worldliness or sins of the flesh. They had meant to be *more* obedient. They were *adding* the teachings of Moses to those of Paul. But by this they were denying that to *Paul*, and *not* to Moses, had been committed the particular message and program *for them*, and for this they were rebuked and called *disobedient:*

"O foolish Galatians, who hath bewitched you, that ye should not obey the truth?" **(Gal. 3:1).**

"Ye did run well; who did hinder you that ye should not obey the truth?" **(Gal. 5:7).**

In seeking to obey Moses, they had *disobeyed* the *truth*, for God had since brought in the dispensation of grace through Paul.

Alas, many today still continue to disobey the truth as they go on under the law.

Indeed, many disobey the truth as they strive in vain to carry out the so-called "Great Commission" with its legalism, its baptismal salvation, its miraculous signs, etc., for God has since given to Paul and to us a greater commission: that of II Corinthians 5:18,19.

We praise God that many who presume to be working under the so-called "Great Commission" do not even try to carry out its details, for if they did they would be still more seriously out of the will of God, but they think only of going into "all the world" with "the gospel." Their failure to see that this commission has been superseded by that later given to Paul, however, only serves to confuse them and those to whom they minister.

How important, then, to remember that while all Scripture was written *for* us; that is, for our *learning* and *profit*, it is not all addressed to us, nor is it all written about us. Our "private mail" is to be found in the epistles of Paul.

CHAPTER V

The Results of Departure from the Pauline Message

Before comparing the messages of Moses and Paul we have yet to enlarge upon the point that, as it was in the case of Moses with Israel, so it is a grievous sin for believers in this dispensation to depart from the message of Paul. In Moses' exhortation to his people, he said:

"When thou shalt beget children, and children's children, and ye shall have remained long in the land, and shall corrupt yourselves, and make a graven image, or the likeness of any thing, and shall do evil in the sight of the Lord thy God, to provoke Him to anger:

"I call heaven and earth to witness against you this day, that ye shall soon utterly perish from off the land whereunto ye go over Jordan to possess it; ye shall

**not prolong your days upon it, but shall
utterly be destroyed.**

**"And the Lord shall scatter you among
the nations, and ye shall be left few in
number among the heathen, whither the
Lord shall lead you" (Deut. 4:25-27).**

The Israelites were not to take their
blessings in Canaan for granted as time
went by, and become indifferent to the
commands of God through Moses. Indeed, Moses warned them, even in his own
day, that if they did this they would soon
"utterly perish from off the land" which
they had gone to possess, and would be
scattered among the heathen.

And so Paul also, in his own day, warned
believers that they would lose the blessings intended for them if they departed
from the truth and the program made
known through him. Indeed, some had
already begun to depart, and the loss of
blessing had immediately become evident.
The Galatians are a striking example of
this—and a lesson to us.

How they had rejoiced when Paul first came to them with "the preaching of the cross" and "the gospel of the grace of God"! As they heard him preach, and noted the difficulty (and perhaps pain) he experienced with his eyes, one said to another: "I wish I could give him *my eyes!* I would gladly do without them. He needs his sight so badly, and think of the joy and blessing he has brought to us!"

But Paul had hardly left them before they were taken in by the Judaizers who "zealously affected [courted]" them to draw them away from Paul and his message (Gal. 4:17).

And now Paul had to write them:

"I marvel that ye are so soon removed from him that called you into the grace of Christ unto another gospel" (1:6).

"O foolish Galatians, who hath bewitched [charmed] you, that ye should not obey the truth, before whose eyes Jesus Christ hath been evidently [plainly] set forth, crucified among you?" (3:1).

43

"Where is then the blessedness ye spake of? **for I bear you record, that, if it had been possible, ye would have plucked out your own eyes, and have given them to me" (4:15).**

The blessedness was gone! Those who had rejoiced together in the riches of God's grace, proclaimed by Paul, had now turned back to Moses and the law. Though God had sent Paul to declare: *"Christ hath redeemed us from the curse of the law"* (3:13) these Galatians had *"desired to be under the law"* (4:9,21) and had left Paul for Moses.

In doing this they *"disobeyed the truth"* (3:1; 5:7) and lost the blessedness for, strangely, while they *"desired* to be under the law"* they did not *"hear the law"* (4:21), but *"bit and devoured one another"* until Paul had to warn them: *"Take heed that ye be not consumed one of another"* (5:15).

Thus it is still today. The Church has lost "the blessedness" (Gal. 4:15) and reaped the "curse" (1:8,9) in the measure that she has forsaken Paul and his message. Her multiplied sects still "bite and devour one another" and are all but "consumed one of another." Even when, professing a desire to *obey* God more perfectly, she goes back to Moses and the law, or to the "Great Commission," she does not *fulfil "the right-eousness of the law"* (Rom. 8:4) nor truly *obey* the "Great Commission." Indeed, she *cannot* carry out the "Great Commission," nor *can* the law ever produce the fruits that grace consistently yields.

Thus the apostle says by authority received from the risen Lord:

"Stand fast therefore in the liberty where-with Christ hath made us free, and be not entangled again with the yoke of bondage.

"Behold, I Paul say unto you...

"Christ is become of no effect unto you, whosoever of you are justified by the law; ye are fallen from grace" (Gal. 5:1-4).

CHAPTER VI

The Messages of Moses and Paul Compared

We now come to a comparison of the teachings of Moses and Paul and see how much it is to our own advantage to understand and obey the message of the glorified Lord to us through Paul, and how much we lose when we depart from that message or confuse it with messages meant for men of other dispensations.

THE LAW VS. GRACE

First, it should be clearly understood that *"the law was given by Moses"* (John 1:17) while to *Paul* was committed *"the gospel of the grace of God"* (Acts 20:24).

We can almost hear some reader object that we have quoted only *part* of John 1:17; that it goes on to say: *"but grace and truth came by Jesus Christ,"* not by Paul. A moment's reflection, however, will reveal the weakness of this objection.

The "law was given by Moses," to be sure, but not at the time of his birth, nor forty years later, when he fled from Pharaoh, nor even forty years after that, when he returned to deliver Israel. It was not until the Passover lamb had been slain and Israel had crossed the Red Sea that Moses ascended Mount Sinai to receive the law from the hands of God. Just so "grace and truth came by Jesus Christ," but not at the time of His birth, nor later, during His earthly ministry, nor even when He died and rose again. It was not until after His death, resurrection and ascension that grace (consistent with truth) came[1] by Jesus Christ—*and He committed the dispensation of it to Paul.*

This could not be stated more plainly than it is in Ephesians 3:1-4:

---

1. *Historically*, as the law was given, historically, by Moses.

48

"For this cause I Paul, the prisoner of Jesus Christ for you Gentiles,

"If ye have heard of *the dispensation of the grace of God which is given me to you-ward:*

"How that by revelation He made known unto me the mystery; (As I wrote afore in few words,

"Whereby, when ye read, ye may understand my knowledge in the mystery of Christ)."

As "the law was given by Moses," then, "the gospel of the grace of God" was committed by the *glorified* Lord to Paul, to dispense to us.

And what a difference!

With Moses, strict obedience was *commanded.* We have seen this in his discourse recorded in Deuteronomy 4. Again and again he refers to "the word which I *command* you." And blessing in the land will require *consistent, continued* obedience too or, he says: *"I call heaven and earth to witness against you this day, that ye shall soon utterly perish from off the land whereunto ye go over Jordan to possess it"* (Deut. 4:26).

How different is the message of grace! There salvation is offered as a *free gift*, on the basis of the finished work of Christ (Rom. 3:25; 6:23) and those who accept the offer and are thus saved, are in turn *exhorted:*

"I beseech you therefore, brethren, by the mercies of God, that ye present your bodies a living sacrifice, holy, acceptable unto God, which is your reasonable service" (Rom. 12:1).

How the apostle himself emphasizes the great contrast between the law with its demands and penalties, and grace with its abundant provision freely bestowed on those who will receive! We quote a few examples:

As to the law, the apostle says, by the Spirit:

"Now we know that what things soever the law saith, it saith to them who

are under the law: *that every mouth may be stopped, and all the world may become guilty before God.*

"Therefore by the deeds of the law there shall no flesh be justified in His sight: for by the law is the knowledge of sin" (Rom. 3:19,20).

"...the law worketh wrath" (Rom. 4:15).

"...the law made nothing perfect" (Heb. 7:19).

He calls the law:

"...the ministration of death" (II Cor. 3:7).

"...the ministration of condemnation" (II Cor. 3:9).

"...the handwriting of ordinances that was against us" (Col. 2:14).

And then he shows grace as the divine complement of the law. What the law *demanded*, grace *provides*:

"Moreover the law entered, that the offence might abound. But where sin abounded, grace did much more abound" (Rom. 5:20).

"...sin shall not have dominion over you: for ye are not under the law, but under grace" (Rom. 6:14).

"For as many as are of the works of the law are under the curse: for it is written, cursed is everyone that continueth not in all things which are written in the book of the law to do them" (Gal. 3:10).

"Christ hath redeemed us from the curse of the law, being made a curse for us" (Gal. 3:13).

"In whom we have redemption through His blood, the forgiveness of sins, according to the riches of His grace" (Eph. 1:7).

"That in the ages to come He might show the exceeding riches of His grace in His kindness toward us through Christ Jesus" (Eph. 2:7).

"And God is able to make all grace abound toward you; that ye, always having all sufficiency in all things, may abound to every good work" (II Cor. 9:8).

"For all things are for your sakes, that the abundant grace might through the thanksgiving of many redound to the glory of God" (II Cor. 4:15).

"I do not frustrate the grace of God: for if righteousness come by the law, then Christ is dead [has died] in vain" (Gal. 2:21).

Mark well; this dispensation of the grace of God was committed to *Paul* by Christ *from His glory in heaven.* The Church, alas, has turned largely to the teachings of Christ *on earth* for her program and has brought untold confusion and division into her midst by her blunder. She has forgotten that Christ on earth was *"made under the law"* (Gal. 4:4) and that He taught His disciples also to be subject to those who sat "in Moses' seat" (Matt. 23:1-3). Some suppose that this was changed after the resurrection, and so strive vainly to carry out our Lord's "Great Commission" to the eleven. But even in this they only bring confusion and division into their ranks, for the program of the "Great Commission" differs widely from that later outlined for us by Christ *in heaven* through the Apostle Paul. Nowhere, in any of the records of our Lord's commission to the eleven do we read anything of *"the dispensation of the grace of God"* or *"the gospel of the grace of God."* Nowhere do we read of *"the preaching of the cross"* (as good news). Nowhere is it revealed that *now* it is no longer necessary to observe Mosaic statutes and ordinances. On the contrary, the eleven were strictly enjoined by the Lord to teach those to whom they were sent that they should *"observe all things whatsoever I have commanded you"* (Matt. 28:20) and the evidence from Acts is clear that under their commission these apostles (now twelve, Acts 1:26) *did* observe the law closely, as their Master had done before them and had commanded them to do.

It was not until Israel had again rejected Christ and His kingdom; until Saul of Tarsus had led his nation in a flaming rebellion against Christ; until sin had *abounded* indeed, that *"grace did much more abound,"* as the rejected Lord reached down from heaven to *save* His chief persecutor and make of him the great example of His matchless grace.

It is because this is so little understood that a bewildered Church has proclaimed a confused "gospel" to a lost world. It is because of this that her "trumpet" has given "an uncertain sound" and her members have not been aroused to "prepare themselves to battle."

GRACE NOT BASED ON COVENANTS

We should note further that whereas Moses enjoined the people of Israel: *"Take heed unto yourselves, lest ye forget the covenant of the Lord your God"* (Deut. 4:23) the Apostle Paul, by the Spirit, bids *us to remember* that we were *not* God's covenant people, but strangers from the covenants; that our blessings are found only *in Christ*, and are based solely on the merits of His finished work:

"Wherefore remember that ye being in time past Gentiles in the flesh....

"That at that time ye were *without Christ*, being *aliens from the commonwealth of Israel*, and *strangers from the covenants of promise*, having *no hope*, and *without God* in the world.

"*But now in Christ Jesus ye who sometimes were far off are made nigh by the blood of Christ*" (Eph. 2:11-13).

To Israel the word was: "Remember the covenant God made with you." To us it is: "Remember that God never made *any* covenant with you; that He grants you salvation and blessing *wholly* by grace."

CANAAN AND THE HEAVENLIES

Next, let us consider the *sphere of blessing* into which God called Israel by Moses, in comparison with that into which He now calls us by Paul.

Moses' instruction to Israel had in view Israel's occupation of *the land of Canaan* and her blessing there. Paul's to us have in view our occupation of *the heavenlies* and our enjoyment of "all spiritual blessings" there.

Even here in Deuteronomy 4 Moses refers repeatedly to *"the land whither ye go to possess it,"* while Paul dwells consistently upon *"the hope which is laid up for you in heaven"* (Col. 1:5).

In the writings of *both* Moses and Paul, however, we find two important elements side by side: *prediction* and *challenge*.

On the basis of the Abrahamic Covenant (Gen. 15:18-21) Moses knew that Israel would one day occupy the land of Canaan and freely *predicted* that this *would* take place (Deut. 33:27-29) but he also knew that in this same covenant God had already deeded to Israel the land of Canaan to be possessed and occupied *by faith.* "Unto thy seed *have I given* this land," is what we read in Genesis 15:18. Thus Moses reminded the covenant people of this challenge as they stood at the threshold of the divine inheritance:

"And I said unto you, Ye are come unto the mountain of the Amorites, which the Lord our God doth give unto us.

"Behold, the Lord thy God hath set the land before thee: *go up and possess it...*" (Deut. 1:20,21).

But, alas, Moses' record goes on to say:

"And ye came near unto me, every one of you, and said, We will send men before us, and they shall search us out the land, and bring us word again by what way we must go up, and into what cities we shall come" (Deut. 1:22).

"Yet in this thing ye did not believe the Lord your God" (Deut. 1:32).

And the result was that the spies (except Joshua and Caleb) returned with the advice that Israel should *not* go up and possess the land (Num. 13:31) and nearly caused the stoning of Joshua and Caleb for insisting that they should. And for that, that whole generation, except Joshua and Caleb, died in the wilderness. This is why Moses later exhorted the new generation in Israel:

"Now therefore hearken...*that ye may live, and go in and possess the land* which

58

**the Lord God of your fathers giveth you"
(Deut. 4:1).**

What a lesson this should be to us as
God sets before us *our* glorious inheritance in the heavenlies!

True, we *shall* someday occupy that
inheritance despite all our failures!

**"For the Lord Himself shall descend from
heaven with a shout, with the voice of the
archangel, and with the trump of God: and
the dead in Christ shall rise first:**

**"Then we which are alive and remain
shall be *caught up* together with them in
the clouds, *to meet the Lord in the air: and
so shall we ever be with the Lord.***

**"*Wherefore comfort one another with
these words*" (I Thes. 4:16-18).**

These are the words of Paul "the apostle of the Gentiles," but like Moses with
Canaan, he offers the heavenlies as more
than a future prospect. He declares that
it is our *present* inheritance; a position we
may *now* occupy *by faith*. Thus in Paul's
writings concerning the heavenlies also

we find the element of *challenge* along with that of *prediction*.

In the Ephesian letter he writes:

"But God, who is rich in mercy, for His great love wherewith He loved us,

"Even when we were dead in sins, *hath quickened us together with Christ*, (by grace ye are saved;)

"And *hath raised us up together, and made us sit together in heavenly places in Christ Jesus*" (Eph. 2:4-6).

This is our position by virtue of our baptism (by the Spirit) into Christ, and it is on the basis of this positional *fact* that the apostle writes to the Colossians:

"*If* [2] *ye then be risen with Christ, seek those things which are above, where Christ sitteth on the right hand of God.*

"*Set your affection on things above, not on things on the earth.*

2. This "if" does not imply doubt as to the fact. It is used entirely by way of challenge, much as a father might say to his twenty-one-year-old son: "If you are twenty-one, why don't you *act* it?"

"For ye are dead, and your life is hid with Christ in God" (Col. 3:1-3).

Oh, that we might make better response to the apostle's challenge than Israel did to that of Moses! The Church as a whole has done no better than Israel. She remains almost totally indifferent to the riches of grace and glory held out to her. Like Israel, she fails to enter in because of unbelief (Heb. 3:19). But her unbelief does not affect the fidelity of God, nor make His Word of none effect (Rom. 3:3). Let *us* therefore, like Joshua and Caleb, accept the challenge of God and say with respect to our inheritance in the heavenlies: *"Let us go up at once, and possess it,"* and so appropriate and enjoy by faith the *"all spiritual blessings in the heavenlies"* which are ours in Christ.

WE ARE GOD'S INHERITANCE

But not only did Israel *receive* an inheritance from God; the favored nation *was* His inheritance as well, for Israel was (and is) to be purified and glorified as His own precious possession.

Thus Moses says:

"But the Lord hath taken you, and brought you forth out of the iron furnace, even out of Egypt, *to be unto Him a people of inheritance, as ye are this day*" (Deut. 4:20).

God, of course, will come into the full *enjoyment* of this inheritance when Israel is finally saved and exalted among the nations, but under Moses there was still the challenge:

"Now therefore, IF ye will obey My voice indeed, and keep My covenant, then ye shall be *a peculiar treasure unto Me above all people*: for all the earth is Mine" (Ex. 19:5).

And so it is with the Church of this dispensation, the Body of Christ. We have *received,* as we say, the riches of grace and glory as our inheritance in Christ, but more: *we* are *Christ's* inheritance as well, and our apostle prays most fervently:

"That the God of our Lord Jesus Christ, the Father of glory, may give unto you the spirit of wisdom and revelation in the knowledge of Him:

"The eyes of your understanding being enlightened; that ye may know what is the hope of His calling, and what *the riches of the glory of His inheritance in the saints*" **(Eph. 1:17,18).**

By grace He will yet make His blood-bought Body the glory of the universe, for it is God's immutable purpose for "the ages to come," to *"show the exceeding riches of His grace in His kindness toward us through Christ Jesus"* (Eph. 2:7).

"...Christ also loved the Church, and gave Himself for it;

"That He might sanctify and cleanse it with the washing of water by the Word,

"That He might present it to Himself a glorious church, not having spot, or wrinkle, or any such thing; but that it should be holy and without blemish" **(Eph. 5:25-27).**

As with Israel, so with us, our Lord will come into the full enjoyment of His inheritance in a future day when we are finally and fully transformed into His likeness. But again, as with Israel, we may *begin* giving Him the joy of His inheritance *now* as we enter into these glorious truths by faith and let them control our lives and transform us into His likeness (II Cor. 3:18).

GOD HATH SPOKEN

There is a passage in Deuteronomy 4 which, at first sight, might make it seem that Israel had one great advantage over us in her relationship to God. It is the following:

"For ask now of the days that are past, which were before thee, since the day that God created man upon the earth, and ask from the one side of heaven unto the other, whether there hath been any such thing as this great thing is, or hath been heard like it?

"Did ever people hear the voice of God speaking out of the midst of the fire, as thou hast heard, and live?" (Deut. 4:32,33).

64

It *was* indeed a great honor and a great privilege that God conferred upon the people of Israel as He spoke to them by word of mouth amid the lightnings and thunders of Sinai. In Israel's case *alone,* "God spake all these words" audibly. Never before had God undertaken to address a nation personally.

Ah, but God has since spoken to *all mankind,* and in an even more striking manner. At Sinai He spoke the words of the law; now, from heaven, He speaks of mercy and grace.

Some suppose that the case is exactly the opposite. They suppose that the absence of miraculous demonstrations, the want of divine intervention in the affairs of men, etc., indicates indifference or "slackness" on God's part, while in fact this apparent indifference speaks to us more eloquently than did the voice of God to Israel at Sinai.

In his epistle to the Hebrews, the apostle declares that:

"God...hath in these last days spoken unto us by [in] His Son...Who...when He had by Himself purged our sins, sat down on the right hand of the Majesty on High" (Heb. 1:1-3).

And today He sits there still, while neither He nor the Father does anything to avenge His brutal murder. God is silent, you say? He refrains from speaking to man? If so, it is only because He has spoken His last word[3] in the person of His glorified Son, who remains at His right hand as the Giver of grace to a lost world, on the basis of His own finished work (Heb. 2:9). This silence is more eloquent than the voice that spoke from Sinai. It cries to sinners everywhere: *"The door of grace is still open. Be reconciled to God while you may. Now is the accepted time. Now is the day of salvation"* (See II Cor. 5:14-6:2). And it cries to saints: *"You still have an opportunity to make the message of grace known to others, though it may not be long.*

---

3. Before speaking again in judgment, Psalm 2:5.

66

Buy up the time; take advantage of the opportunity, because the days are evil" (See Eph. 5:16).

As Sir Robert Anderson has well said:

"A silent heaven! Yes, but it is not the silence of callous indifference or helpless weakness. The silence is the pledge and proof that the way is open for the guiltiest of mankind to draw near to God. When that silence is broken one day it will mean the withdrawal of the amnesty; the end of the reign of grace; and the dawning of the day of wrath foretold in Scripture. God is silent now because He has spoken His last word of mercy and love in Christ. He is beseeching men to be reconciled (II Cor. 5:20). The One to whom all judgment has been committed, and who will appear one day as the Judge of all, is now the Savior and is seated upon the Father's throne in grace."

SO VERY NEAR

There is another passage in Deuteronomy 4 which falls into somewhat the same category as that which we have just considered. It is that in which Moses says to his people:

"For what nation is there so great, who hath God so nigh unto them, as the Lord our God is in all things that we call upon Him for?" (Deut. 4:7).

This was indeed true, for God *was* near to the people of Israel. He had directed Moses, while still in the mount:

"...let them make Me a sanctuary; that I may dwell among them" (Ex. 25:8).

And now He *did* dwell among them in the tabernacle.

As we further examine the record, however, and compare it with the teachings of Paul as to the intimate relationship which now exists between God and the members of Christ's Body, the "nearness" of God to Israel seems almost like "farness."

It must not be supposed that God dwelt openly with His people or that they had free access to Him at all times.

He dwelt, as we have said, in the tabernacle. Indeed, He dwelt within its innermost sanctuary—the Most Holy Place, or the Holy of Holies—which was shut off from the rest of the tabernacle by a thick "veil" or curtain.

Not everyone could enter the Holy of Holies. *Only a priest* might do this. Nor could *all* priests enter; only *one,* the *high* priest. And even *he* could not enter whenever he wished, but *only once each year*, at the prescribed time. Nor, even then, could he simply enter the presence of God, for he must bring with him *the blood* of the sacrifice. Thus we read in Hebrews 9:7,8:

"But into the second [the Most Holy Place] went *the high priest alone once every year, not without blood*, which he offered for himself, and for the errors of the people:

"The Holy Ghost this signifying, that the way into the holiest of all was NOT yet made manifest...."

Thus, while God indeed dwelt nearer to Israel than to any other people of that time, He still kept Himself at a distance from even them.

It is not so with us. There is no barrier whatever between God and His people today, for in the great Pauline revelation we find that the humblest member of the Body of Christ has been *"made accepted in the Beloved [One]"* (Eph. 1:6) has a position before God *"complete in Him"* (Col. 2:10) and, by virtue of his baptism into Christ, has been *made to sit in the heavenlies at God's right hand* (Eph. 2:6; Col. 3:1-3) there to be *"blessed with all spiritual blessings"* (Eph. 1:3).

Thus our *position* is, and remains, a heavenly one, simply because we are "in Christ." We may not always *occupy* this position experientially, or *appropriate* and *enjoy* our blessings in the heavenlies, but the *position* remains the same. God *always* sees us *in Christ* at His right hand (See Rom. 8:1,31-34, R.V.).

70

But even *experientially* we are brought much nearer to God than Israel ever was. To the *Hebrew* believers who had trusted Christ when Israel was set aside because of her unbelief, Paul wrote, by inspiration:

"Having therefore, brethren, boldness to enter into the holiest by the blood of Jesus,

"By a new and living way, which He hath consecrated for us, through the veil, that is to say, His flesh" (Heb. 10:19,20).

Some have supposed that this cannot refer to members of the Body since they are *already seated in God's presence* in Christ. But our *position* must not be confused with our *experience* and *privilege*. Ephesians, the same epistle which teaches us that we *are seated* at God's right hand, *also* teaches that we have *access* into His presence (i.e., *experientially)*. Writing to Gentile believers, but writing *about* both Jewish and Gentile believers, Paul says, by the Spirit:

"And [He] came and preached peace to you which were afar off, and to them that were nigh.

"For through Him *we both have access* by one Spirit unto the Father" (Eph. 2:17,18).

In Romans 5:1,2 our *standing* and our *privilege* are spoken of together:

"Therefore *being justified* by faith we have peace with God through our Lord Jesus Christ:

"By whom also *we have access* by faith into this grace wherein we stand...."

How near God has brought us to Himself! In Christ we have already been brought into His presence. In our daily experience "we have *access* by faith into this grace wherein we stand"!

As we read the words of Moses: *"What nation is there who hath God so nigh unto them?"* we may well consider the more intimate nearness of God to Christ and the members of His Body, and sing with deepest gratitude:

Near, so very near to God,
Nearer I cannot be,
For in the person of His Son
I am as near as He.

A TESTIMONY TO ANGELS AND MEN

Let us observe further how Moses exhorted Israel to bear testimony to the nations round about as to the wisdom of obeying the law and how, by comparison, Paul bids us bear testimony to men *and angels* as to the wisdom of *God's purpose* in dealing with us on the basis of *grace.*

To Israel Moses said:

"Keep therefore and do them [these statutes and judgments]; for this is your wisdom and your understanding in the sight of the nations, which shall hear all these statutes, and say, surely this great nation is a wise and understanding people" (Deut. 4:6).

To us, the Apostle Paul declares by the Spirit that God has made known "the mystery,"

73

"To the intent that now unto the principalities and powers in heavenly places might be known by the church the manifold wisdom of God" (Eph. 3:10).

When it is understood that the mystery was God's answer to Satan's attempts to render the fulfillment of prophecy impossible, this statement becomes the more deeply significant. It explains, too, why Paul wrote of himself:

"...We have become a spectacle to the world, both to angels and men" (I Cor. 4:9, New Tr.).

PROVISION FOR SPIRITUAL VICTORY

There is more than *testimony,* however, involved in the exhortations of Moses and Paul. Moses admonished his people to be ready for *war* against the nations determined to keep them out of their land though, he assured them, it was God's purpose to give them the victory:

"To drive out nations from before thee greater and mightier than thou art, *to*

bring thee in, **to give thee their land for an inheritance, as it is this day" (Deut. 4:38).**

So Paul, by the Spirit, also admonishes us to be ready for war; not against "flesh and blood" but against Satan and his hosts, who would keep us from *occupying* (experientially) our position and appropriating our blessings in the heavenlies.

"For our wrestling is not against flesh and blood, but against the principalities, against the powers, against the spiritual hosts of wickedness in the heavenly places" (Eph. 6:12, R.V.).

But, as with Israel, so with us, it is God's will that we have the victory, and have it we may—*by faith.* The believer need not always be defeated. Indeed God has made gracious provision for victory in *every* battle. He has given us His "whole armor" (Gr. *panoply, "full suit of armor")* that we may "withstand" and, after the battle, be found still standing, as He goes on to say:

"Wherefore take up the whole armor of God, that ye may be able to withstand in

**the evil day, and, having done all, to stand"
(Ver. 13, R.V.).**

Clearly, this armor is complete and sufficient for *victory in every case*, for it includes *no protection for the back.* It is complete *without* protection for the back, for the one who wears it need never turn and flee.

Amazing thought! that God has equipped us to put Satan and the fallen angels to flight and to drive them out so that we may occupy their place in the heavenlies!

Like failing Israel, the Body of Christ has largely failed to put her foes to flight and occupy her rightful inheritance in the heavenlies, God will finally have to do it for *both* Israel and the Body *wholly by grace.*

For us, the members of the Body, the Lord will come with "*a shout*," with "*the voice of the archangel*" and with "*the trump of God*," and catch us away, through the hosts of wickedness, to be with Him

(I Thes. 4:16,17). This all speaks of war, or at least preparedness for war. And there will be war indeed—war in heaven itself, before it is all over, when God takes things in hand and casts Satan out of his long-held possession (Rev. 12:7-9) so that we may come into the fullness of it.

In closing, the fact that the Church as a whole has failed to "take the land," does not mean that we must individually fail, for to *the individual members* of the Body the apostle cries: "...My brethren, BE STRONG IN THE LORD...Put on the whole armor of God that ye may be able to STAND...that ye may be able to WITHSTAND in the evil day, and having done all, to STAND. STAND THEREFORE...."

BIBLE INDEX

BIBLE INDEX

The Berean Searchlight

The *Berean Searchlight* is the outgrowth of a small church bulletin containing brief weekly Bible lessons by Pastor C. R. Stam in 1940. Its publication has become the largest and most important function of the *Berean Bible Society*, reaching monthly into every state of the Union and more than 60 foreign countries.

The *Searchlight* includes in its mailing list thousands of ministers, missionaries and other Christian workers. Also, it is on display in the libraries of hundreds of Christian Colleges and Bible Institutes. The purpose of the *Berean Searchlight* is to help believers understand and enjoy the Bible.

Send for our FREE Bible Study Magazine today!

BEREAN BIBLE SOCIETY
PO Box 756
Germantown, WI 53022

www.bereanbiblesociety.org

Our Great Commission

By C. R. Stam

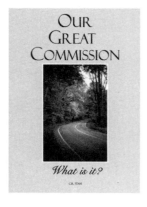

PAPERBACK

142 PAGES

SCRIPTURE INDEX

The commission our Lord gave the eleven has been called "The Great Commission" for so long that multitudes of sincere believers think *the Bible* calls it that. But this designation reflects traditional views, and "the traditions of men" all too often "make void the Word of God." Granted, this was a *great* commission, but the ascended Lord later committed a far *greater* message and ministry to Paul.

Orders:

Berean Bible Society, PO Box 756,
Germantown, WI 53022

www.bereanbiblesociety.org

Things That Differ

By Cornelius R. Stam

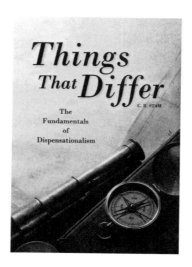

This volume demonstrates how the dispensational method of Bible study is the method God approves, and the only one by which the Bible makes sense. It shows the perfect harmony between the changeless principles of God and His changing dispensations.

HARDCOVER   **290 PAGES**

Orders:

Berean Bible Society
PO Box 756
Germantown, WI 53022

www.bereanbiblesociety.org

Berean Bible Society
Germantown, WI

The **Purpose** of the *Berean Bible Society* is to help you understand and enjoy the Bible. The **Mission** of BBS is to exalt the Lord Jesus Christ by proclaiming the whole counsel of God according to the revelation of the Mystery. Our **Goals** are to *evangelize* the lost, to *educate* the saved in "rightly dividing the Word of truth" (II Tim. 2:15), to *energize* their Christian lives, and to *encourage* the local church.

- The Society publishes the ***Berean Searchlight***, a Bible study magazine that is sent out monthly free of charge.

- BBS offers a wide selection of **literature**, CDs, and DVDs, on various subjects to help believers grow in grace.

- BBS arranges **Bible Conferences** for the study of God's Word, rightly divided and to evangelize the lost.

- **CDs** or **audio tapes** are provided through our free lending library for personal use and Bible classes.

- ***"Two Minutes with the Bible,"*** is featured in newspapers across the country and is sent out as a daily email.

BEREAN BIBLE SOCIETY
PO Box 756, Germantown, WI 53022

www.bereanbiblesociety.org